COLOR *and* FRAME

coloring book for adults

BIBLE VERSES

Illustrated by Lynn Melchiori

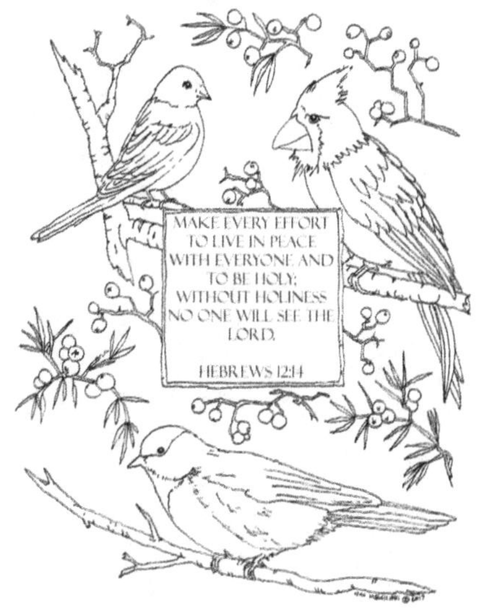

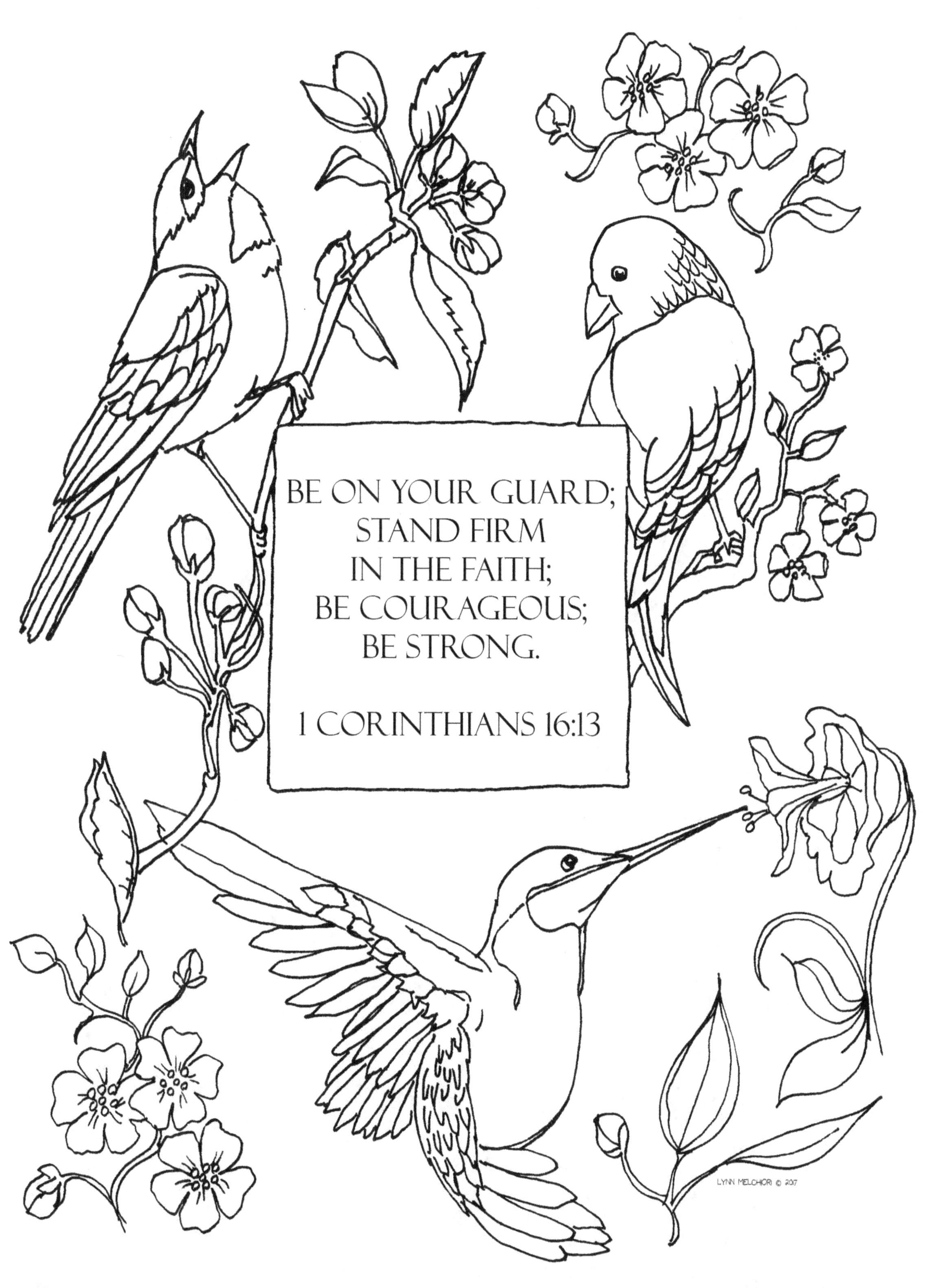

BE ON YOUR GUARD;
STAND FIRM
IN THE FAITH;
BE COURAGEOUS;
BE STRONG.

1 CORINTHIANS 16:13

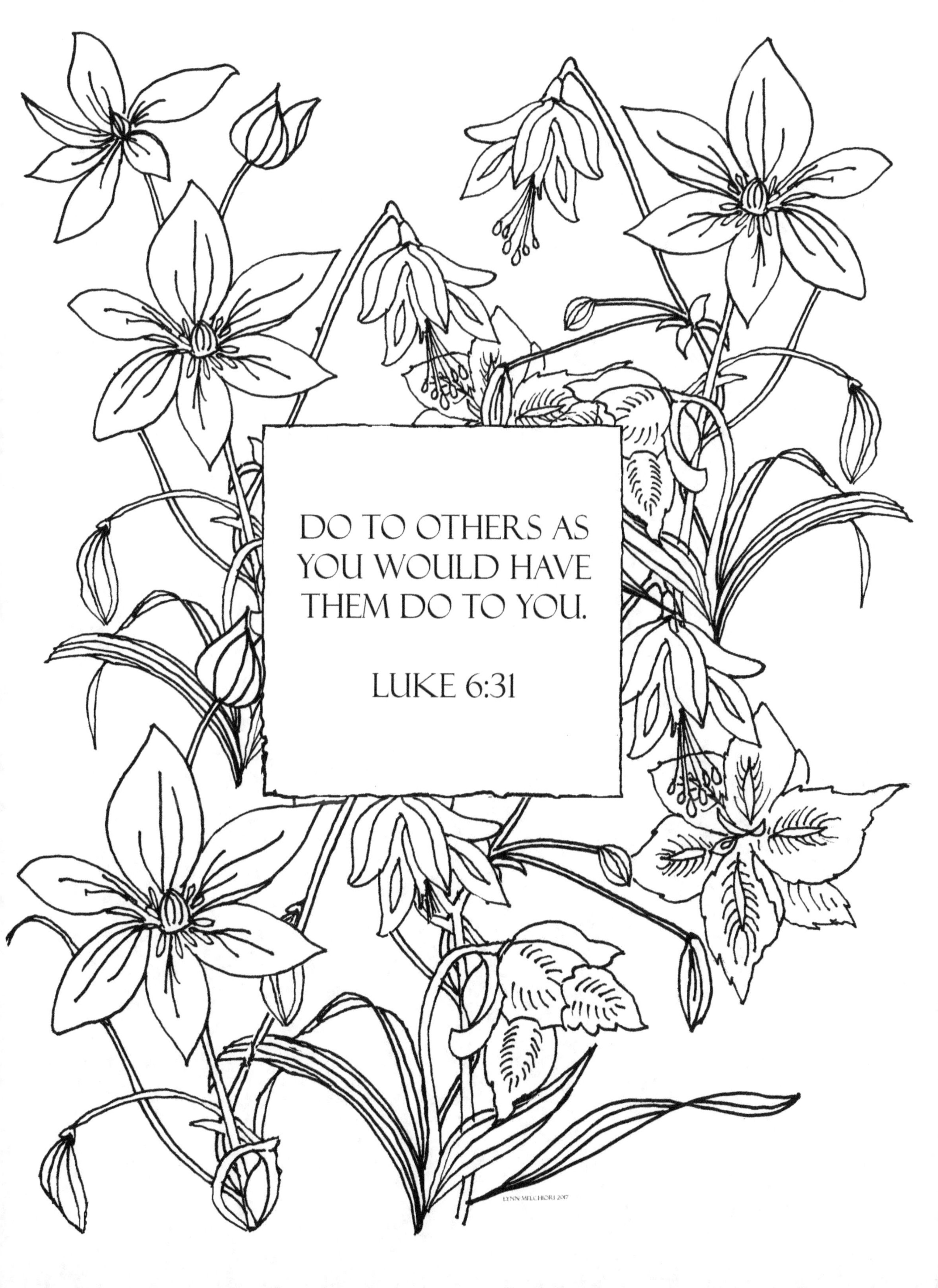

DO TO OTHERS AS
YOU WOULD HAVE
THEM DO TO YOU.

LUKE 6:31

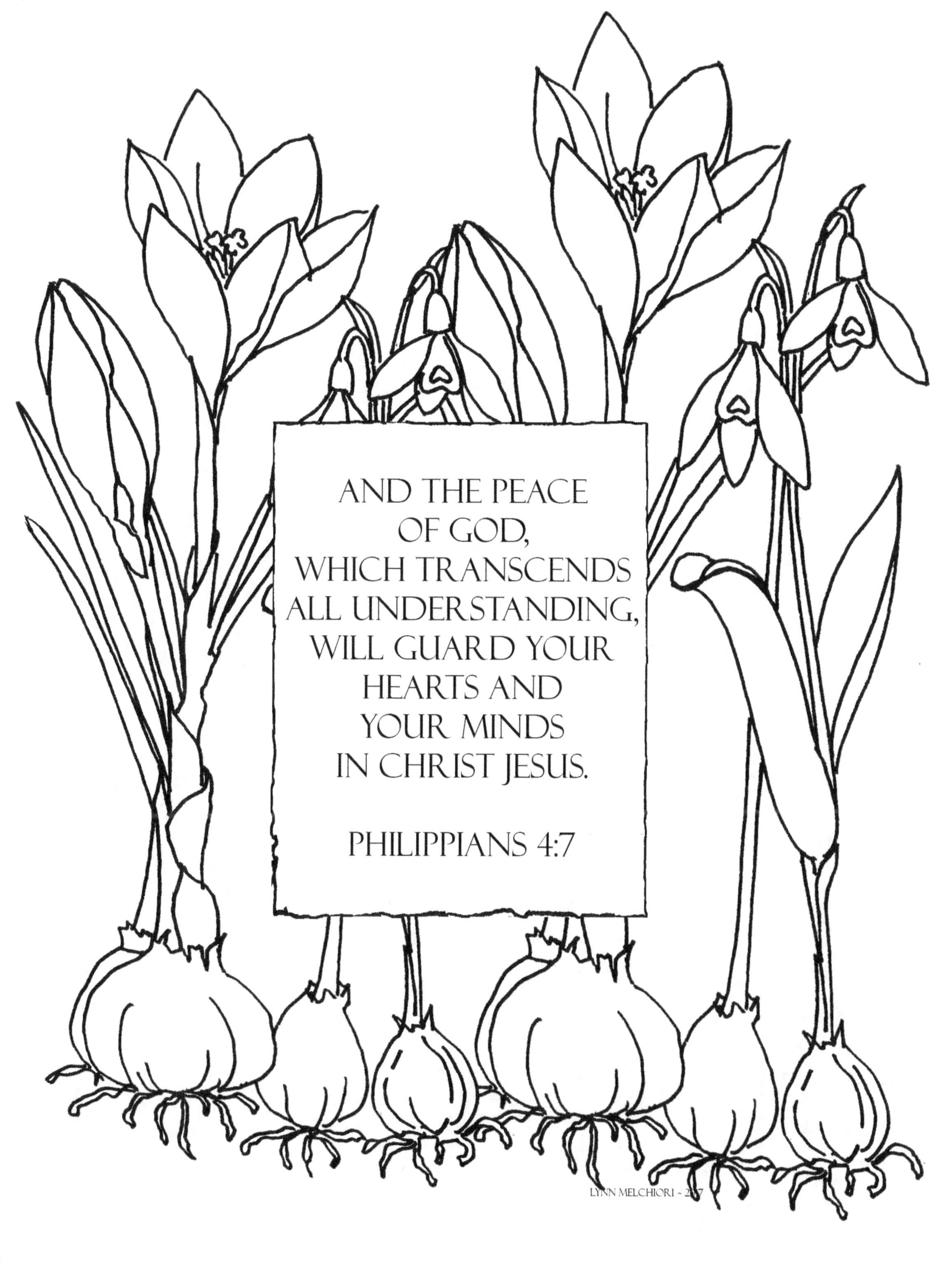

AND THE PEACE
OF GOD,
WHICH TRANSCENDS
ALL UNDERSTANDING,
WILL GUARD YOUR
HEARTS AND
YOUR MINDS
IN CHRIST JESUS.

PHILIPPIANS 4:7

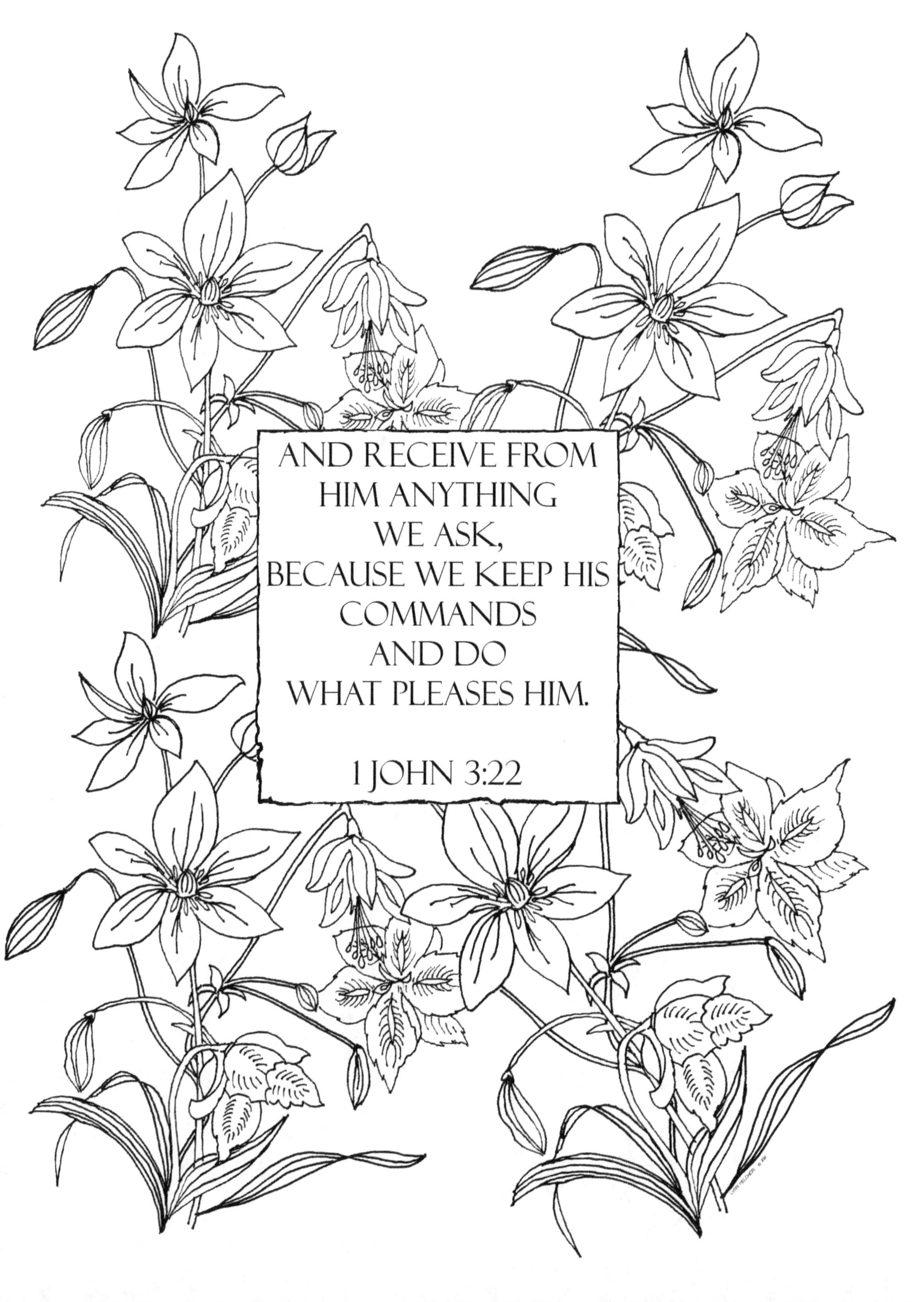
AND RECEIVE FROM
HIM ANYTHING
WE ASK,
BECAUSE WE KEEP HIS
COMMANDS
AND DO
WHAT PLEASES HIM.

1 JOHN 3:22

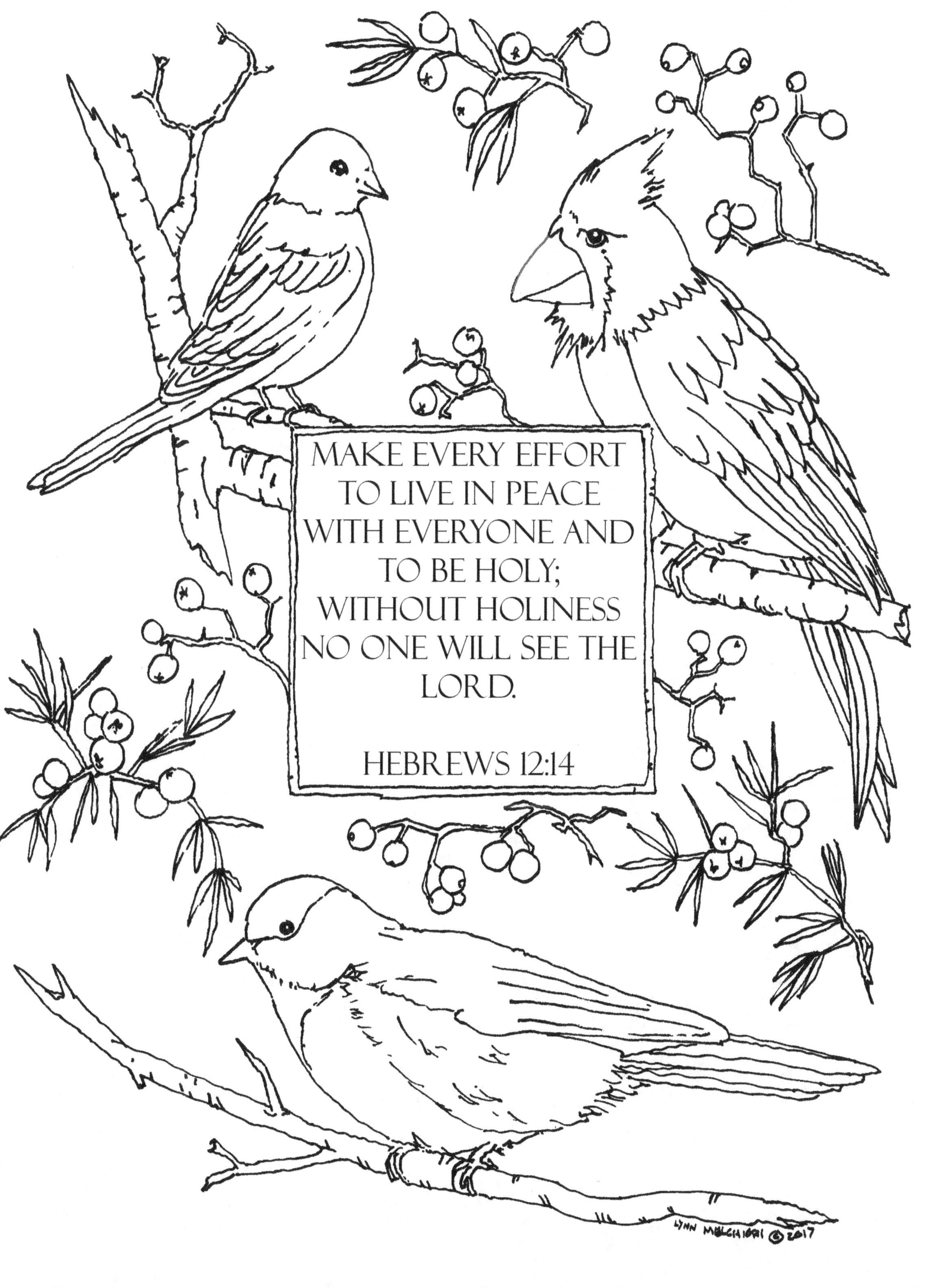

MAKE EVERY EFFORT
TO LIVE IN PEACE
WITH EVERYONE AND
TO BE HOLY;
WITHOUT HOLINESS
NO ONE WILL SEE THE
LORD.

HEBREWS 12:14

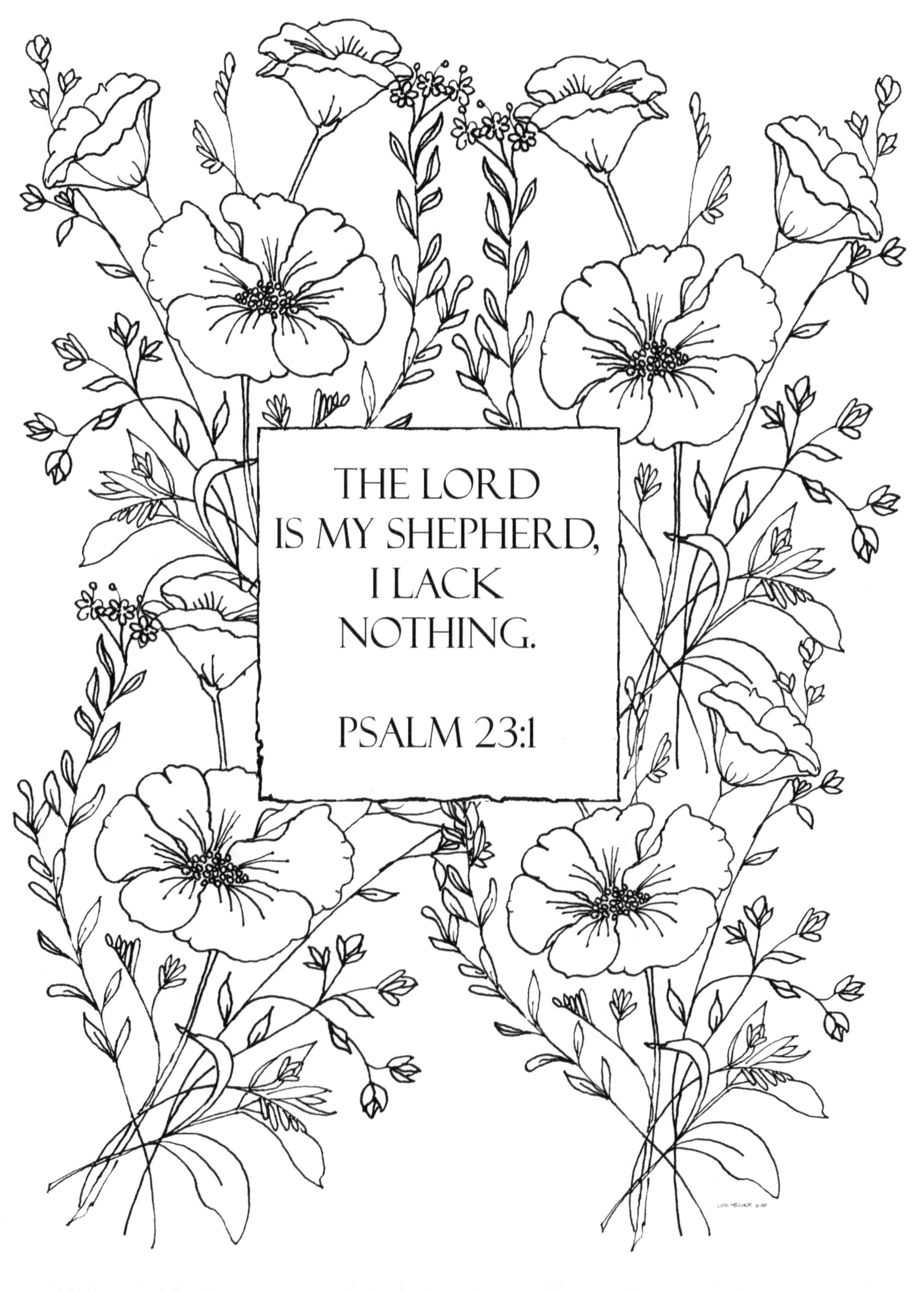

THE LORD
IS MY SHEPHERD,
I LACK
NOTHING.

PSALM 23:1

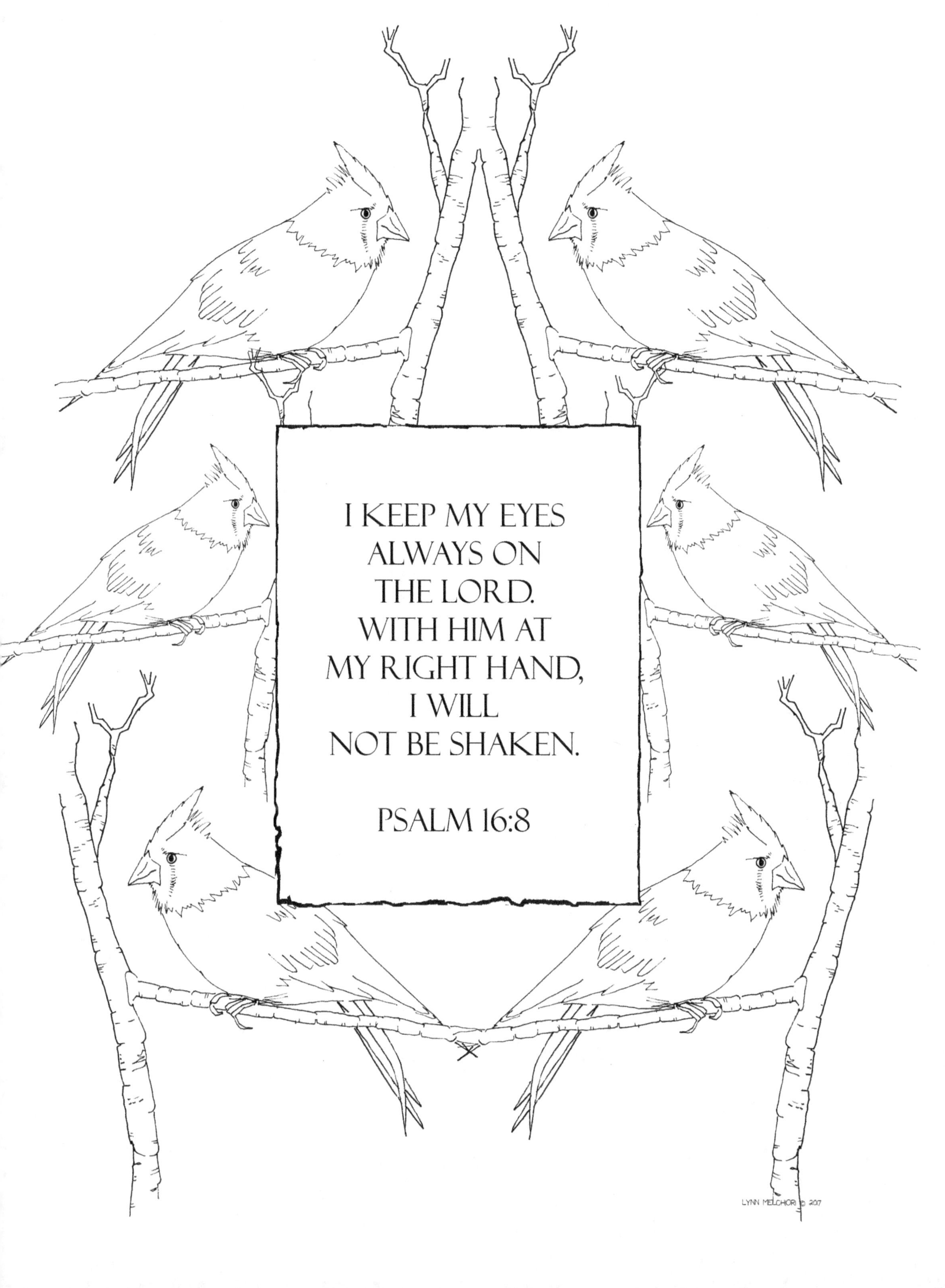

I KEEP MY EYES
ALWAYS ON
THE LORD.
WITH HIM AT
MY RIGHT HAND,
I WILL
NOT BE SHAKEN.

PSALM 16:8

LYNN MELCHIOR © 2017

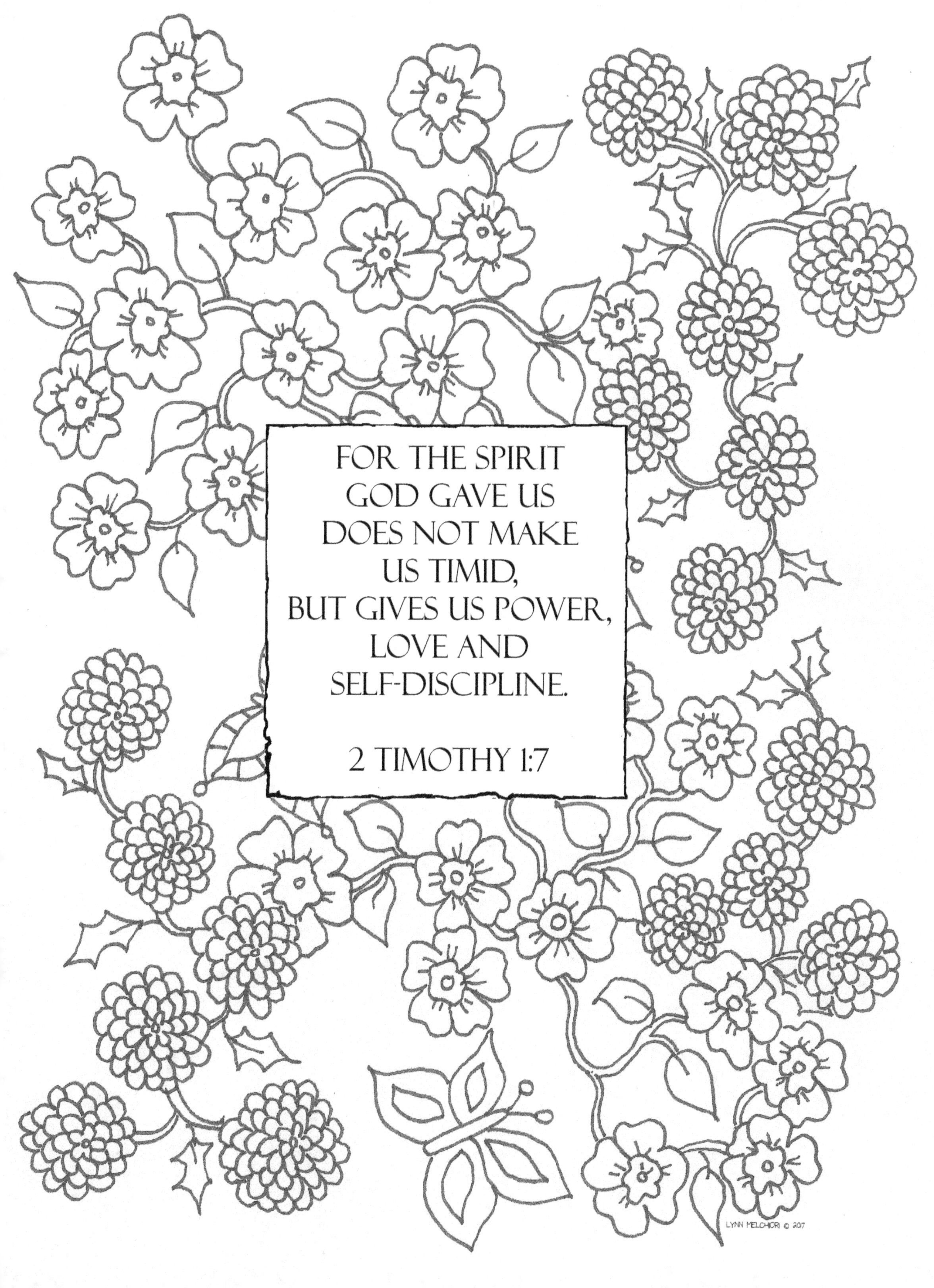
FOR THE SPIRIT
GOD GAVE US
DOES NOT MAKE
US TIMID,
BUT GIVES US POWER,
LOVE AND
SELF-DISCIPLINE.

2 TIMOTHY 1:7

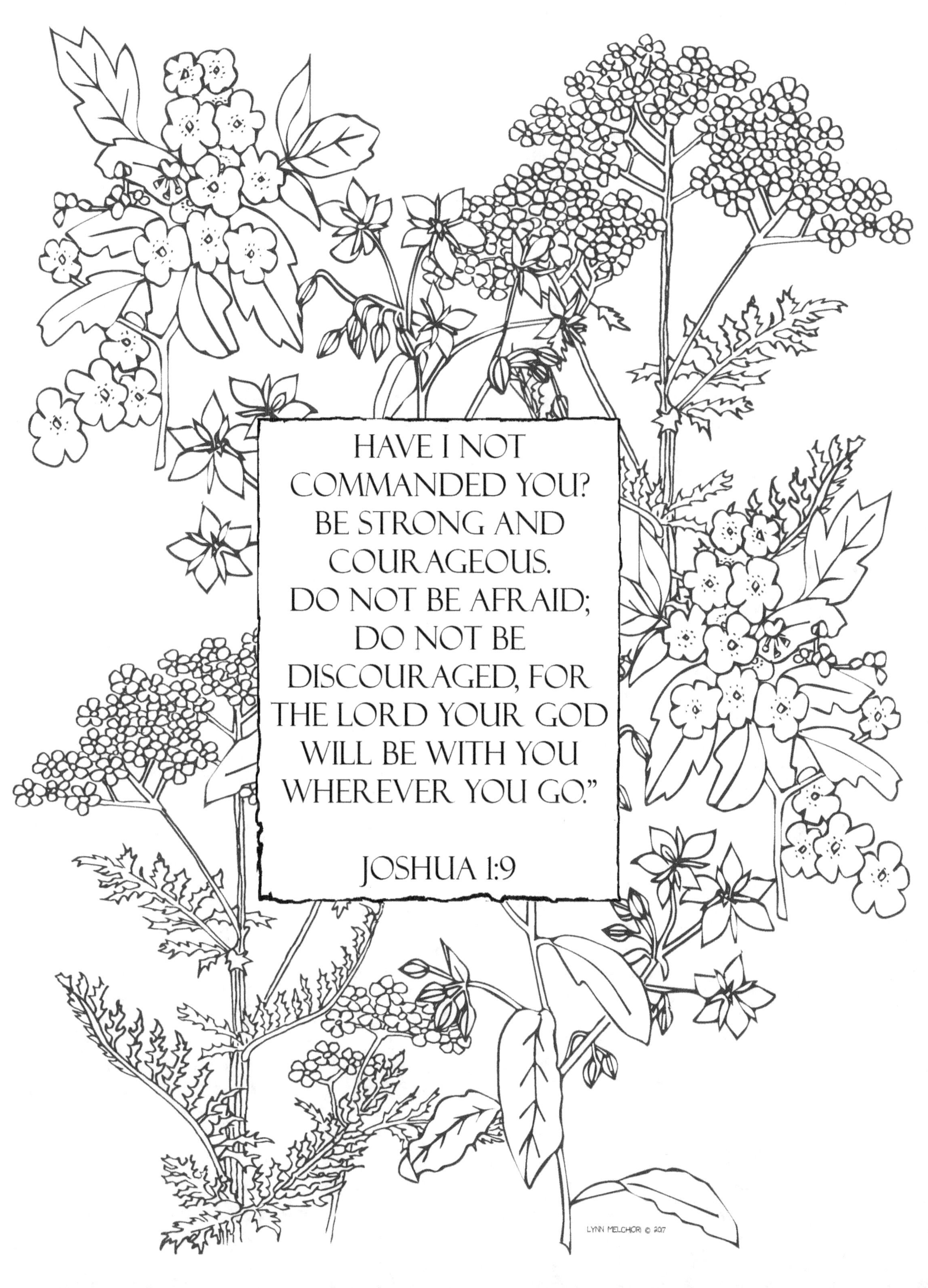

HAVE I NOT
COMMANDED YOU?
BE STRONG AND
COURAGEOUS.
DO NOT BE AFRAID;
DO NOT BE
DISCOURAGED, FOR
THE LORD YOUR GOD
WILL BE WITH YOU
WHEREVER YOU GO."

JOSHUA 1:9

LYNN MELCHIORI © 2017

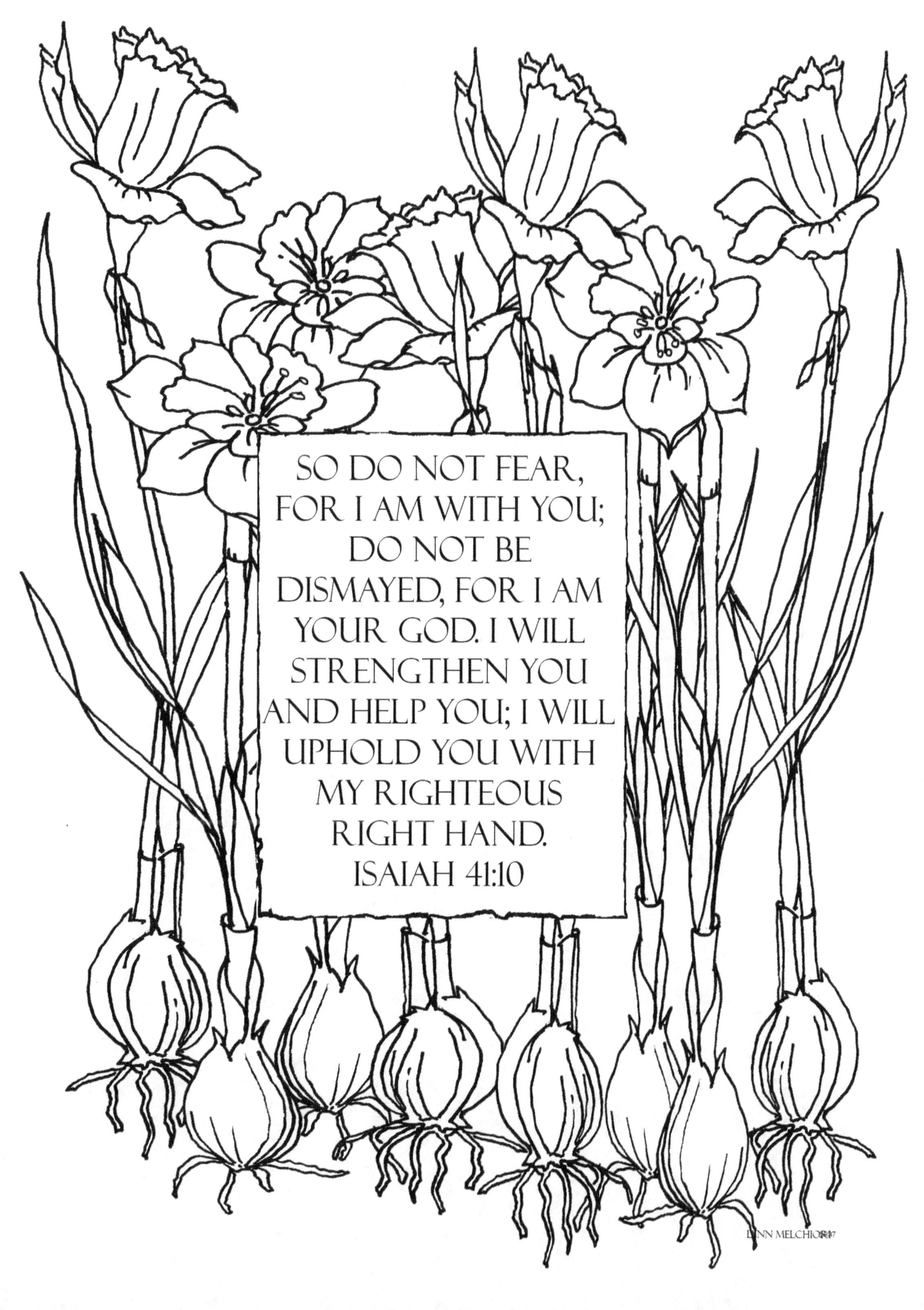

SO DO NOT FEAR,
FOR I AM WITH YOU;
DO NOT BE
DISMAYED, FOR I AM
YOUR GOD. I WILL
STRENGTHEN YOU
AND HELP YOU; I WILL
UPHOLD YOU WITH
MY RIGHTEOUS
RIGHT HAND.
ISAIAH 41:10
LYNN MELCHIOR '17

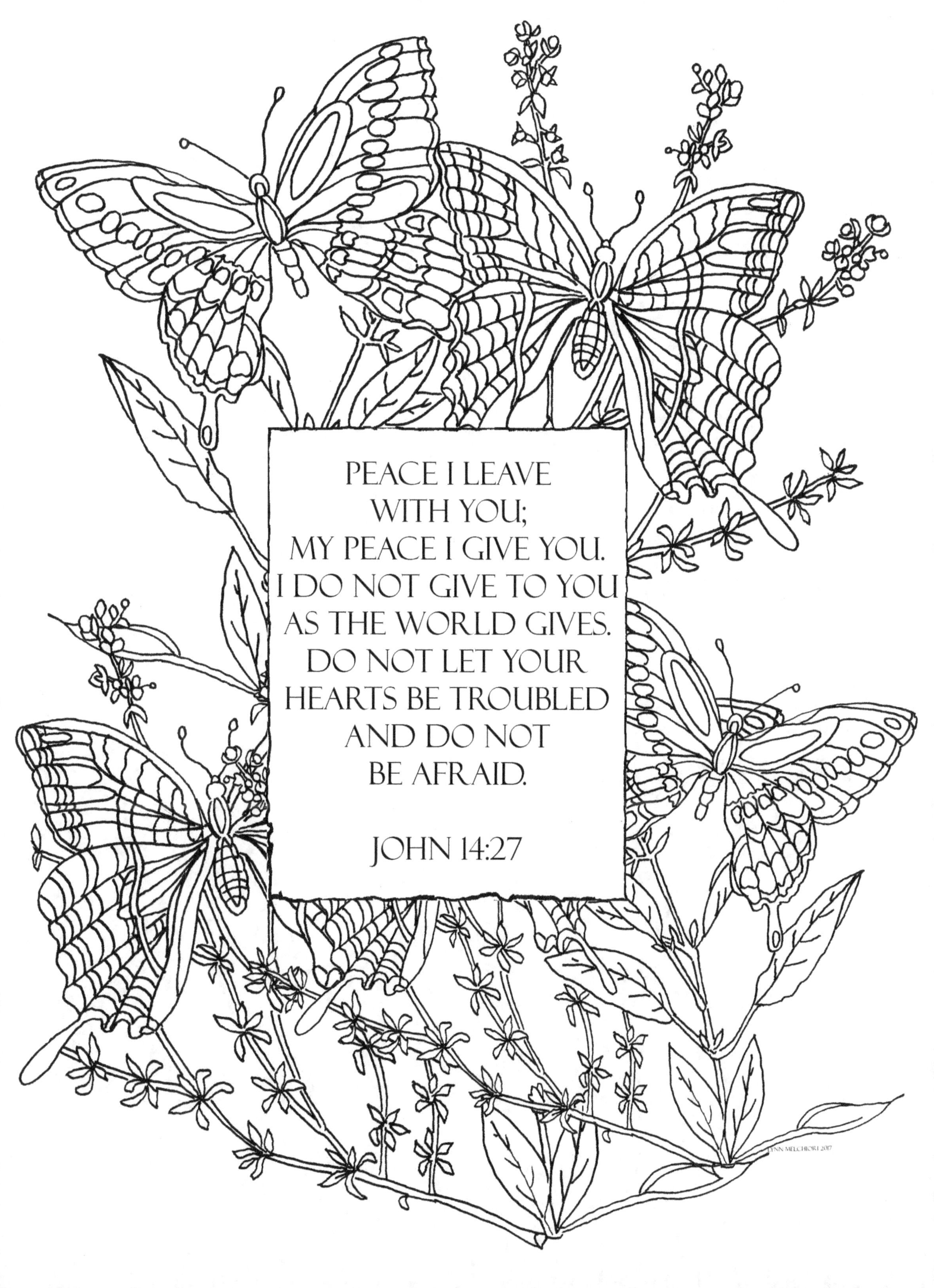

PEACE I LEAVE
WITH YOU;
MY PEACE I GIVE YOU.
I DO NOT GIVE TO YOU
AS THE WORLD GIVES.
DO NOT LET YOUR
HEARTS BE TROUBLED
AND DO NOT
BE AFRAID.

JOHN 14:27

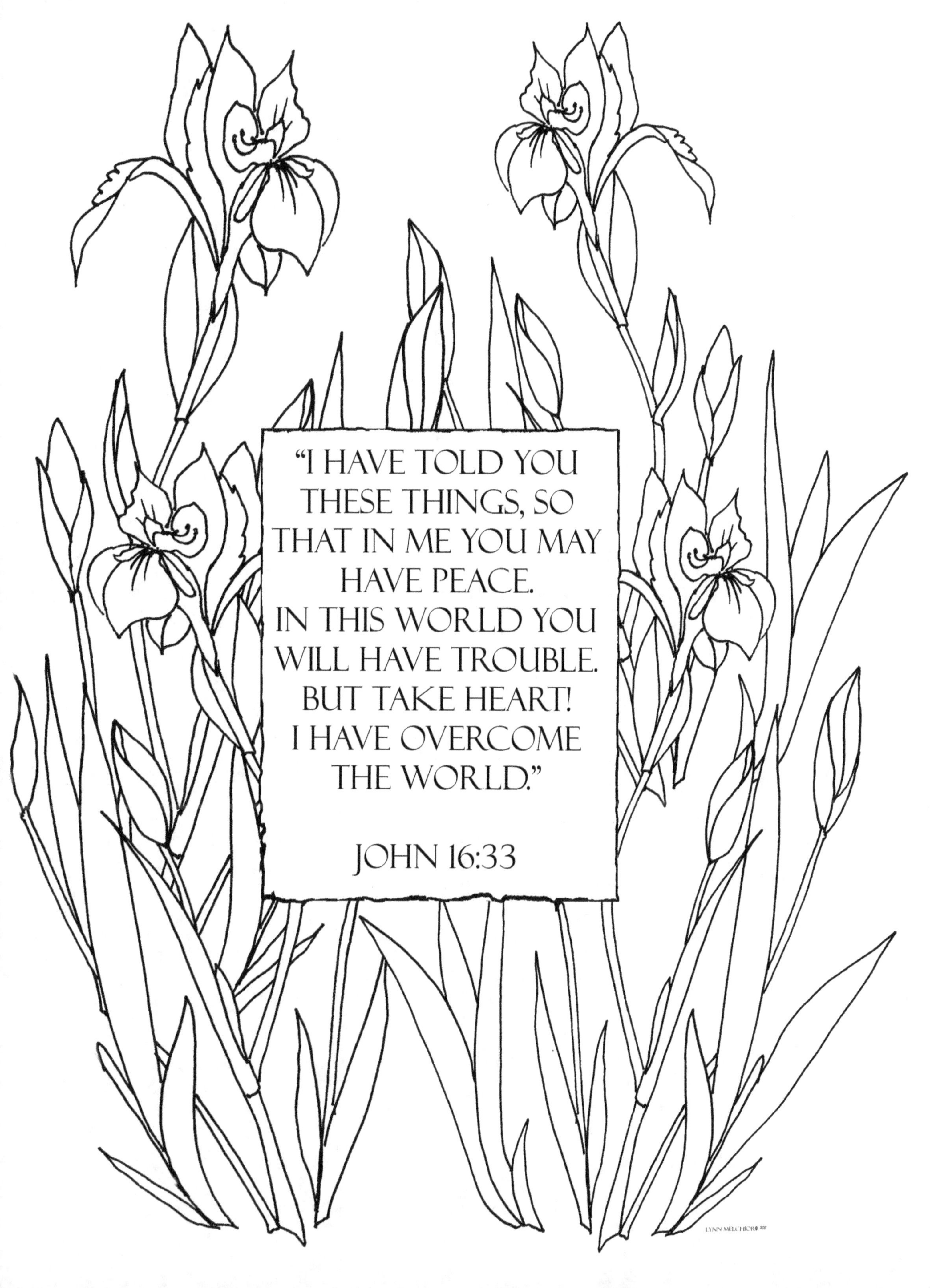

"I HAVE TOLD YOU THESE THINGS, SO THAT IN ME YOU MAY HAVE PEACE. IN THIS WORLD YOU WILL HAVE TROUBLE. BUT TAKE HEART! I HAVE OVERCOME THE WORLD."

JOHN 16:33

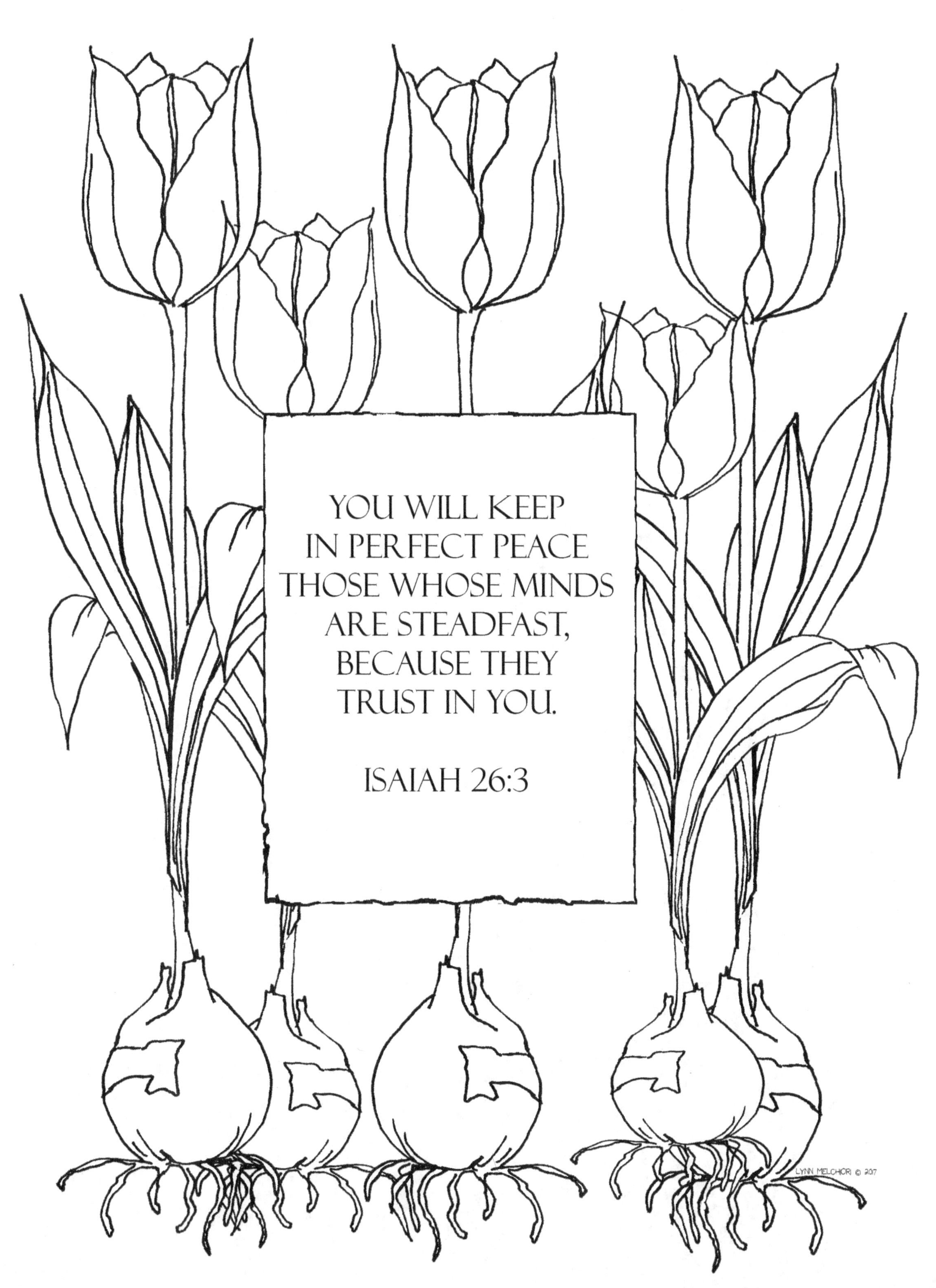

YOU WILL KEEP
IN PERFECT PEACE
THOSE WHOSE MINDS
ARE STEADFAST,
BECAUSE THEY
TRUST IN YOU.

ISAIAH 26:3

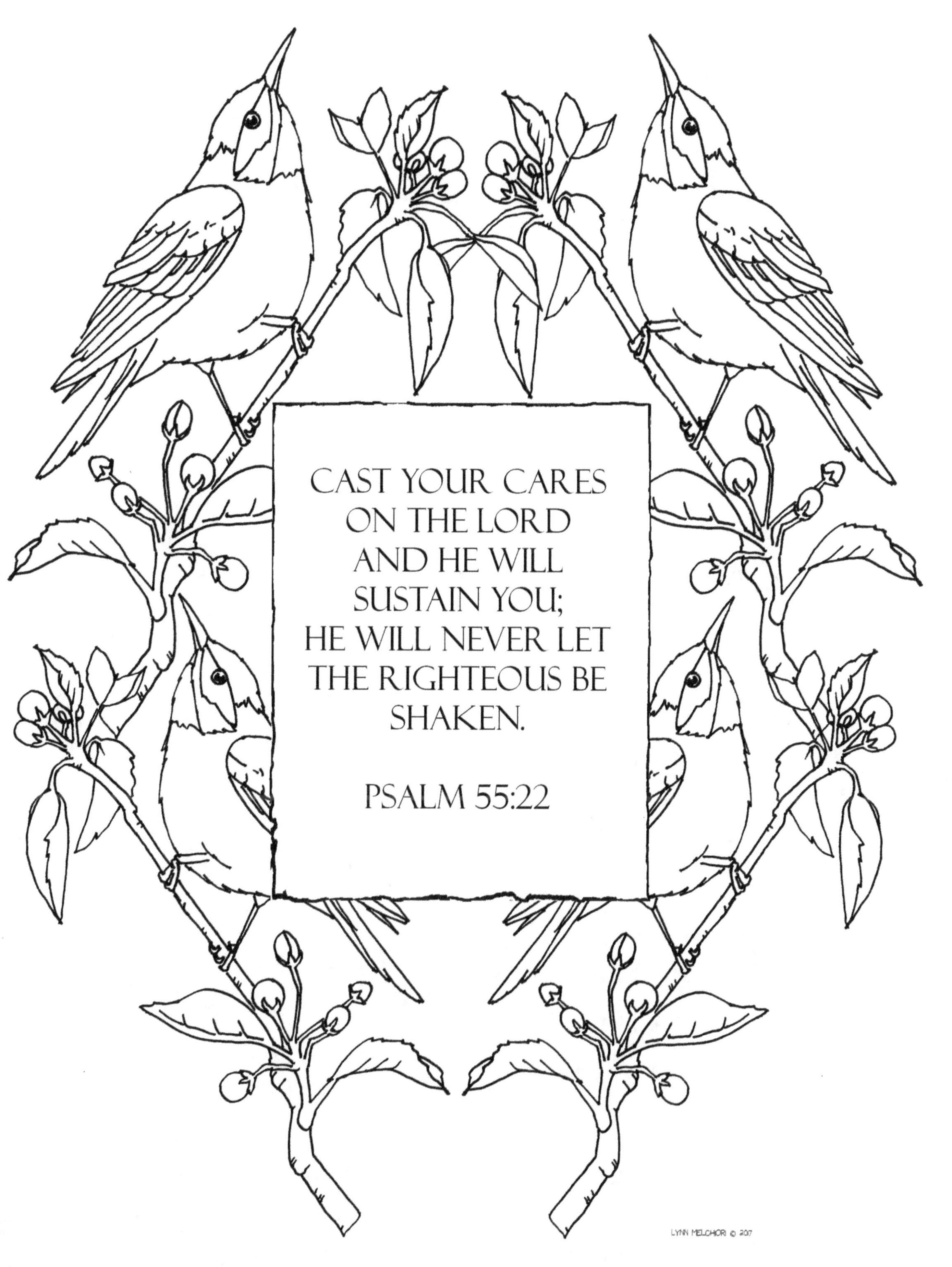
CAST YOUR CARES
ON THE LORD
AND HE WILL
SUSTAIN YOU;
HE WILL NEVER LET
THE RIGHTEOUS BE
SHAKEN.

PSALM 55:22

LYNN MELCHIORI © 207

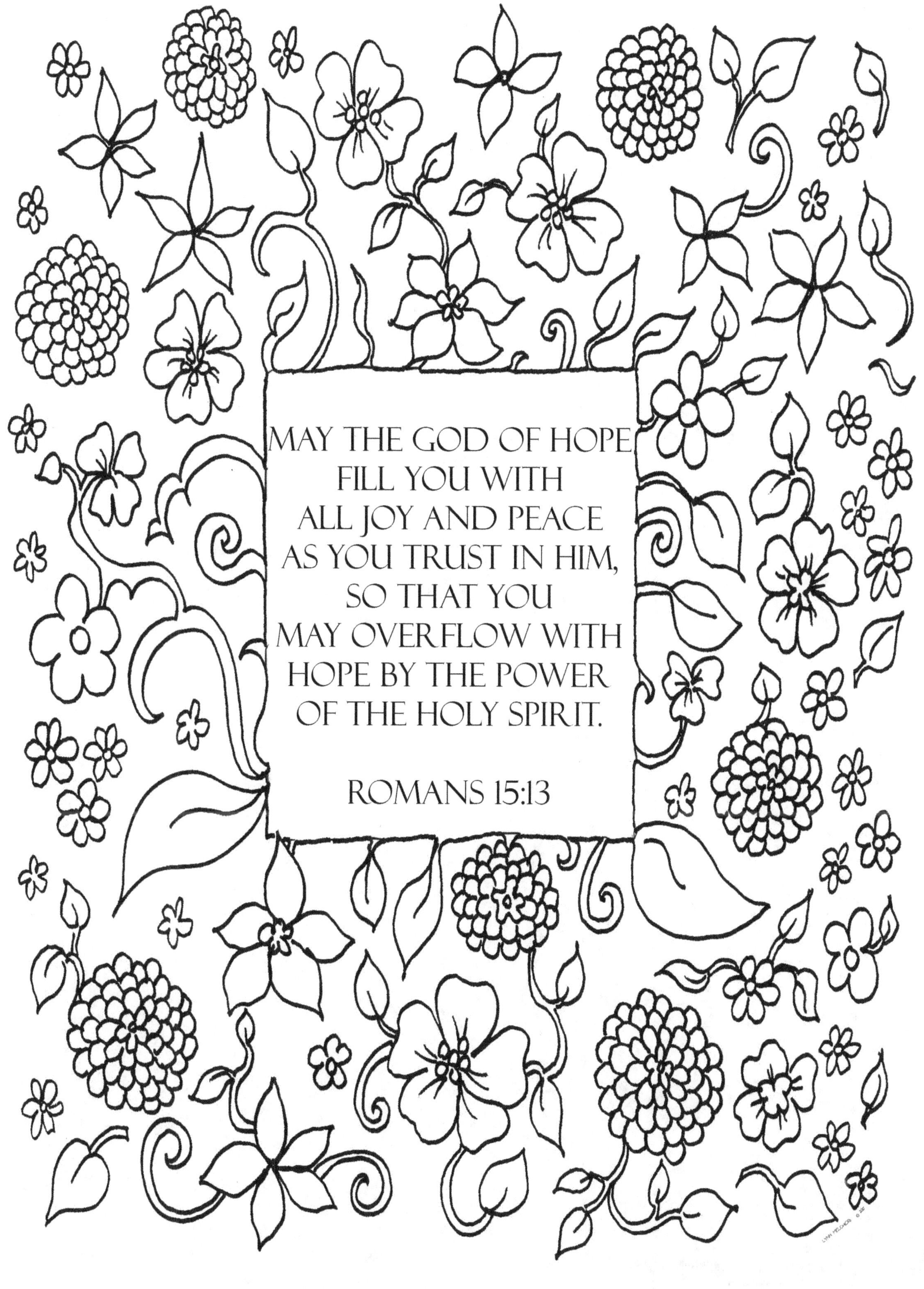

MAY THE GOD OF HOPE
FILL YOU WITH
ALL JOY AND PEACE
AS YOU TRUST IN HIM,
SO THAT YOU
MAY OVERFLOW WITH
HOPE BY THE POWER
OF THE HOLY SPIRIT.

ROMANS 15:13

www.ingramcontent.com/pod-product-compliance
Lightning Source LLC
Chambersburg PA
CBHW080507030726
47592CB00011B/3281